THE PENITENCE OF ADAM

CORPUS

SCRIPTORUM CHRISTIANORUM ORIENTALIUM

EDITUM CONSILIO

UNIVERSITATIS CATHOLICAE AMERICAE

ET UNIVERSITATIS CATHOLICAE LOVANIENSIS

Vol. 430

SCRIPTORES ARMENIACI

TOMUS 14

THE PENITENCE OF ADAM

TRANSLATED

BY

MICHAEL E. STONE

LOVANII

IN AEDIBUS E. PEETERS

1981

ISBN 2-8017-0168-8

D/1981/0602/6

Imprimerie Orientaliste, s.p.r.l., Louvain (Belgique)

INTRODUCTION

THE ADAMIC LITERATURE

The *Penitence of Adam* is an Armenian version of a work preserved in numerous languages. Before examining its particular character, the other versions should be mentioned.[1] They are in Greek (entitled *Apocalypse of Moses*);[2] Latin (entitled *Vita Adae et Evae*);[3] Slavonic (entitled *Life of Adam and Eve*)[4] and Georgian (entitled *Life of Adam*).[5] The Latin, Greek and Slavonic versions have been translated into European languages, notably English and German.[6] The Georgian version has never been translated.

Each of these five writings, in Latin, Greek, Slavonic, Georgian and Armenian, is a different recension of the Adam book. Each of them contains unique materials, distinctive structural elements and its own particular terminology. Yet they also share much text and many traditions. The relationships between them, then, are complex and are not decisively clarified by the publication of the Armenian *Penitence of Adam*. Still, observations on certain particular points relevant to this problem will be made below.[7] Wells who edited the Greek, Latin and Slavonic versions in R.H. Charles' *Apocrypha and Pseudepigrapha of the*

---

[1] For bibliographical and introductory information, see the following works: A.M. DENIS, *Introduction aux pseudépigraphes grecs d'Ancien Testament* (SVTP 1; Leiden: Brill, 1970), 3-14; J.H. CHARLESWORTH, *The Pesudepigrapha and Modern Research* (SCS 7; Missoula: Scholars, 1976), 72-75; H. ANASYAN, *Armenian Bibliology* I (Erevan; Academy, 1959), 236-250 (Armenian); M.E. STONE, "Report on Seth Traditions in the Armenian Adam Books," *The Rediscovery of Gnosticism*, ed. B. Layton, II (SHR 41; Leiden: Brill, 1980), 460-464 (forthcoming).

[2] C. VON TISCHENDORF, *Apocalypses Apocryphae* (repr. Leipzig: 1966), 1-23; additional collations in M. NAGEL, *La vie grecque d'Adam et d'Ève* (dissertation, Strassburg: 1972), Part 2: "L'édition des textes".

[3] W. MEYER, *Vita Adae et Evae* (München: K. Adademie, 1897).

[4] V. JAGIČ, "Slavische Beiträge zu dem biblischen Apokryphen, I, Die altkirchenslavischen Texte des Adamsbuches," *Denkschr. K. Akad. Wiss. philos.-hist. Classe 42* (Vienna: 1893).

[5] Ts. K'URTSIK'IDZE, in *Philological Studies I* (Tiflis: Academy, 1964), 97-136 (Georgian).

[6] See standard editions of the Pseudepigrapha. Jagič (note 4, above) includes a German translation with his edition.

[7] The chief aim of Nagel's thesis (note 2, above) is to clarify this relationship.

Old Testament regarded the Greek *Apocalypse of Moses* as the chief story line to which certain additions were made in the Latin and Slavonic versions.[8]

In addition to the five versions, three further sources for the text of the Adam book survive. The first is the Armenian translation of the *Apocalypse of Moses*. It was published by Yovsēp'ianc' and translated into English by Issaverdens.[9] Yovsēp'ianc' did not use all the manuscripts of this book and some of the others were listed by Anasyan.[10] It is entitled *Book of Adam* and is a direct textual witness of the *Apocalypse of Moses*. It was compared with the *Penitence of Adam* and no relationship was found between the two writings at the Armenian level. The second source is the *Gospel of Nicodemus* (the *Acts of Pilate*) which contains a substantial section of the text. The third source is a Greek fragment containing the story of the repentance of Adam and Eve, an incident not found in the *Apocalypse of Moses*.[11]

Here a few observations are added on the Georgian *Life of Adam*, the least known of the versions. These are drawn from the introductory comments by K'urtsik'idze. He uses five manuscripts, two of the seventeenth century and three of the nineteenth century. A supposed tenth-century testimony to the Georgian *Life of Adam* is a reference by Euthymius of Athos to a book of this name.[12] It is by no means certain, however, that Euthymius is referring to the same work. K'urtsik'idze also suggests that the *Life of Adam* may have been included in one of the recensions of the *Primary History of Georgia*.[13] Kekelidze is of the view that the work was translated into Georgian from Armenian prior to the tenth century.[14] The Georgian *Life of Adam* appears, from what is known of it, to be close to the Armenian *Penitence of Adam*. Our examination of a small sample of text suggests, however, that the extant Armenian work is not the direct source of the Georgian writing. Clearly,

---

[8] Vol. 2 (Oxford: 1913), 128-129.

[9] S. YOVSĒP'IANC', *Uncanonical Books of the Old Testament* (Venice: Mechitarist, 1896), 1-23 (Armenian); J. ISSAVERDENS, *Uncanonical Writings of the Old Testament* (2 edn; Venice: Mechitarist, 1934), 23-42.

[10] Anasyan (note 1, above), 238 lists five copies in Erevan. Note also Jerusalem, Armenian Patriarchate nos. 256, 1278, and apparently 1729, 2043. Other copies doubtless exist.

[11] Vat. Gr. no. 1192, 13r-14v, cf. Denis (note 1, above), 4; Nagel (note 2, above), 175 ff. This has been utilized in our own transcription.

[12] K'urtsik'idze (note 5, above), 97.

[13] Ibid., 99-100.

[14] Ibid., 103-108.

now that the Armenian *Penitence of Adam* has become known, a detailed study of the relationship between the two texts is desirable.[15]

Distinct from the above writings are the numerous Adamic tales found in many languages. These include writings in Syriac, Ethiopic, Arabic, Georgian and Slavonic, as well as in Armenian. These works often contain developments of themes, ideas and incidents found in the Adam book. Many of these Adamic writings have been consulted in the course of preparation of the annotations to the translation of the *Penitence of Adam*. None of them, even those in Armenian, has a special literary or other relationship with the *Penitence of Adam*, although frequently parallels or similarities in one or another specific detail are noted.[16]

The Armenian Adamic writings also bear upon the *Penitence of Adam* in another way. The most recent list enumerates thirteen Armenian Adamic writings, not counting the *Penitence of Adam* itself, and more of them will probably be discovered.[17] There are also numerous poetic, liturgical and homiletic writings in Armenian devoted to Adam and his deeds.[18] This extensive literature provides a context within which the *Penitence of Adam* was preserved and transmitted. The Armenians cherished and developed, embellished and passed on legends and tales about biblical characters, and Adam, the protoplast, was particularly dear to them. The spelling out of the implications of this for the history of Armenian thought must await the full publication and study of the Armenian Adamic writings.

The close relationship between the *Penitence of Adam* and the Georgian *Life of Adam* was noted above. Lüdtke has described the contents and character of a number of other Georgian Adamic works which seem to be very similar to certain Armenian Adamic writings. The whole subject is hardly investigated, but a clarification of this relation-

---

[15] The Georgian *Life of Adam* was apparently not known to W. LÜDTKE, "Georgische Adam-Bücher," *ZAW* 38 (1919), 155-168.

[16] Much information on the various Adamic writings is to be found in the works cited in note 1, above and in Lüdtke's article cited in note 15, above. We have distinguished versions of the (putative) Adam book from other Adamic writings, even though some of them may also derive in one respect or another from the same "Adam book". In certain cases the distinction is more one of the degree of departure from the putative source document than one of kind. The five versions are much closer to one another than any of them is to works like the *Cave of Treasures* or the Ethiopic *Book of Adam and Eve*.

[17] Stone (note 1, above), 460-464

[18] Anasyan (note 1, above), 245-248 lists twenty six such compositions.

ship might well illuminate that between the Georgian *Life of Adam* and the Armenian *Penitence of Adam*.[19]

GENERAL STRUCTURE OF THE BOOK

The work opens in a fashion similar to the *Latin Vita Adae et Evae* giving the story of Adam and Eve's repentance after their expulsion from the Garden of Eden, of their standing in the Jordan and Tigris Rivers, and of Satan's renewed enticement of Eve. It follows the general story line of the Latin *Vita Adae et Evae*, and is to a very considerable extent similar to it, up to the point where the *Apocalypse of Moses* commences.

From the point where the *Apocalypse of Moses* commences, the *Penitence of Adam* can be compared with the Greek and Armenian versions of that work as well as with the Latin *Vita Adae et Evae*. This comparison shows that while the *Penitence of Adam* bears a clear overall resemblance to the *Apocalypse of Moses*, it also has very numerous points of agreement with the *Vita Adae et Evae*. Such agreements include phrases, verses and even more extended passages or traditions. In addition to material which the *Penitence of Adam* has in common with *Apocalypse of Moses* and the Latin *Vita Adae et Evae*, it has a good deal of material peculiar to itself. This is usually included in the formulation of verses which from a structural view point are parallel to material to be found in the Greek and Latin works, but are, in form, content or emphasis, quite different. The occurrence of additional, rather than substitute material, is less frequent.

The *Penitence of Adam* does not contain two of the blocs of special material which occur in the Latin *Vita Adae et Evae*, but not in the *Apocalypse of Moses*, viz. the Vision of Adam (*Vita Adae et Evae* 25-29) and Eve's directives as to the memorials of her life (*Vita Adae et Evae* 49-50). It does contain the major account of Eve's fall which is found in the *Apocalypse of Moses* 15-34, but which is absent from the *Vita Adae et Evae*.

THE TITLE

The title *Penitence of Adam* is attested in ancient sources and confusion has surrounded the identification of the works it denotes. The *Decretum Gelasianum* (line 296) records as *Liber Apocryphus* a certain

---

[19] Lüdtke (note 15, above), 155-160.

Liber qui appellatur Paenitentia Adae. It seems unlikely, however, that this refers to our *Penitence of Adam;* more probably it means the *Vita Adae er Evae*. The *Vita Adae et Evae* deals at length with the repentance of Adam and Eve and it was known in Latin, the language of the Gelasian decree, which does not refer to it by any other title. Moreover, the *Vita Adae et Evae* occurs under the titles *De Penitentia Adam* and *Penitentia Adam et Eva* in some manuscripts.

In the *Chronographies* of George Cedrenus and George the Syncellus there is a quotation from an Adamic work. It opens with the words Ἀδὰμ τῇ ἑξακοσιόστῳ ἔτει μετανοήσας ἔγνω δι᾽ ἀποκαλύψεως. In them, both E. Renan and M.R. James saw a possible reference to the title of the chronographers' source, the *Penitence of Adam*. It is, of course, possible that their source was called *Penitence of Adam*, but that is far from being the necessary implication of their words. Indeed, the Syriac versions of the work they cite call it the *Testament of Adam*.[20]

The 12th century Armenian historian, Samuel of Ani in his *Chronography* for the year 590 deals with books introduced into Armenia by Nestorian missionaries. The first in his list is Ահամայ Կտակն "Testament of Adam"; so Erevan manuscript 1869 (1585-1589 C.E.) and Zarbhanalian, while the Vałašapat edition of 1893 reads Ահամայ Ապաշխարութիւն "Penitence of Adam".[21] The latter reading is probably secondary, but it witnesses to the knowledge of a *Penitence of Adam* in Armenian. Otherwise, the change from *Testament* cannot be explained; no *Testament of Adam* is known in Armenian.[22]

Yovsēp'ianc' published in 1896 an Armenian work titled Պատմութիւն Ապաշխարութեան Ահամայ և Եւայի նախաստեղծի թէ որպէս արարին : *The History of the Repentance of Adam and Eve the Protoplasts and What They did*.[23] At points this work is clearly dependent on the Armenian

---

[20] E. RENAN, *Fragments du livre gnostique intitulé: Apocalypse d'Adam ou Pénitence d'Adam ou Testament d'Adam*, extrait du *JA* 17 (1853), separatim 4 f.; M.R. JAMES, *Apocrypha Anecdota* (TS 2.3; Cambridge: 1893), 139. See also IDEM., *The Lost Apocrypha of the Old Testament* (London: SPCK, 1920), 1-3.

[21] The witness of the oldest MS, Jerusalem 1801, written in 1187, i.e. within a decade of Samuel's death, must await the facsimile edition being prepared in Erevan for his 900th anniversary.

[22] The text of Samuel's list is edited by Anasyan (note 1, above), I, xxxix. Line 8 of the text is զիաթեկն i.e. διαθήκη. This does not necessarily refer to a *Testament of Adam*; thus we differ from the views of Zahn, James and Russell, see D.S. RUSSELL, *The Method and Message of Jewish Apocalyptic* (Philadelphia: Westminster, 1964), 394-395, and references there. These scholars, of course, only knew the 1893 edition of the *Chronography*.

[23] Yovsēp'ianc' (note 9, above), 325-330; English by Issaverdens (note 9, above);

week. The Syncellus reads : τῇ ἕκτῃ ἡμέρᾳ τῆς δευτέρας ἑβδομάδος
... λαβὼν ὁ Θεὸς μέρος τι τῆς πλευρᾶς τοῦ Ἀδὰμ ἔπλασε τὴν
γυναῖκα. This point lacks altogether in the Latin *Vita Adae et Evae.*
Chap. 7 And the hair of his head was uncovered.

The Armenian text may be compared with Slav. 36 "even up to the
hair of his head." It is moreover closer to Vat. Gr. 1182, 13v καὶ ἡ
θρὶξ τῆς κεφαλῆς αὐτοῦ ἡπλούτου (sic) τῷ εὐχουμένῳ ἐν τῇ ὕδατι.
Latin *Vita Adae et Evae* lacks all mention of the hair.
Chap. 22 (1) Ap' at whom the nurse named and called Abel.

The Armenian *Book of Adam* translating the *Apocalypse of Moses* has
the name բարեկենդ.[27] The Latin *Vita Adae et Evae* and the Georgian
Life of Adam have no names of this type. The *Apocalypse of Moses*
relates the birth of both brothers at this point and it gives them two
names each. The Latin *Vita Adae et Evae*, the Georgian *Life of Adam*,
and the *Penitence of Adam* relate the birth of Cain in chap. 21 and the
birth of Abel here. In the *Penitence of Adam* Abel has two names, but
Cain does not. Some scholars have seen a relationship between Cain's
colour in the Latin and Armenian versions (chap. 21 *lucidus* or "colour
of the stars") and the name Ἀδιάφωτος given him by Greek *Apocalypse
of Moses* 1. The midwife referred to here may be compared with the
angelic midwife attending the birth of Cain in chap. 21 of the
Armenian *Penitence of Adam*. Georgian refers to the midwife as "the
power of God", cf. "two powers" in Armenian *Penitence of Adam* 21.
Latin has no reference to a midwife here.
Chap. 44 (16) Armenian Greek

Armenian	Greek
"Why do you worship Adam every morning? You came into being before him. Why is it that you, who are the former one, worship the latter? Why do you worship (Adam) or (why) are you fed by Adam and are not fed by the fruit of Eden?	Why dost thou eat of Adam's tares and not of Paradise?

The narrative from which this excerpt is drawn is not extant in Latin
Vita Adae et Evae. Nearly all Greek MSS have an additional phrase
preceding the sentence quoted here, viz. ὅμως προσκυνεῖς τὸν

---

[27] On this point see M.E. STONE, "Apocryphal Notes and Readings," *Israel Oriental Studies* 1(1971), 126.

ἐλαχίστερον; The phrase is the same found in the Armenian *Penitence of Adam* "worship the latter". Greek seems to have lost the preceding material by corruption. Wells' comment that the Greek words are a gloss from chap. 14 of the *Vita Adae et Evae* is superfluous. Instead, the parallel with chap. 14 of the Latin and Armenian is very revelant. There Satan explains that he rebelled against God's command to bow down to Adam because he was former. Here, in the Armenian *Penitence of Adam*, Satan uses exactly the same argument to incite the serpent to rebellion. So Armenian clearly preserves the text lying behind the Greek phrase. Furthemore, its full implication is only clear in the forms of the book which include the repentance story, such as the Latin *Vita Adae et Evae* and the Armenian *Penitence of Adam* itself.

Chap. [44] (20) and I stood by the tree.

Greek reads καὶ ἐστὶν παρ' αὐτῶν τῶν φυτῶν.

Arm obviously reflects ἔστην. This is a clear indication that it had a Greek *Vorlage*. Arm is also probably original; it makes better sense and avoids the awkwardness of the Greek.

The Search for Food

Chaps 1-9 contain a recurrent theme of Adam and Eve's search for food such as they had eaten in the Garden. Their original food is contrasted with "the food of grass" which was appointed for the animals (cf. Gen. 1:29-30 and 3:18). This theme is mentioned in the *Vita Adae et Evae*, but it is far more explicit in the *Penitence of Adam*. Thus it occurs in it in chaps 4, 6 and 8, in which it does not occur in the *Vita Adae et Evae*. Chap. 8 may serve as an example. Adam calls on the fish of the Jordan to mourn with him and observes:

Latin	*Armenian*
non se plagnant sed me, *quia ipsi non peccaverunt sed ego,*	and bewail me, not for their own sakes, but for mine. *Because God did not withold their food from them which God appointed from the beginning, but I have been withheld from my food and from life.*

In the *Penitence of Adam* the intimate connection between the search for paradisical food and repentance is clear. The expulsion from the Garden meant a separation from their food. Only the protoplasts' repentance or God's mercy might perhaps bring about its restoration. In

tion to orthodox Christology in the very role attributed to Christ. The view is of Adam's resurrection, his purification from his sins by a ritual bath in the Jordan, and subsequent anointing; Adam, the first man, is the first man thus redeemed, and his salvation is the prelude to the salvation of all men, who are to be anointed (but not, or at least we are not told about it, baptized).

A literary consideration also bears on the comparison of these two passages. The speech of the angel comes in response to Seth's request for the oil. In the Latin text, the anointing of Adam is not mentioned explicitly and the last phrase, stating that he will be brought to the tree of mercy, although perhaps implying anointing, is almost by way of an afterthought. In the Armenian text, however, Adam's future anointing at the hands of Michael forms the central point of the passage. Michael, who refuses Seth the oil in the present, promises himself to anoint Adam in the future. This makes the Armenian text far more responsive tò the demands of the broader literary context.

Thus, this passage seems to be more primitive than the extant texts of the *Vita Adae et Evae* and of the *Apocalypse of Moses*. Moreover the unusual ideas in it seem to stem from Christian sectarian circles. Yet this is not the only case in which the *Penitence of Adam* seems to be more primitive than either the Latin *Vitae Adae et Evae* or the Greek *Apocalypse of Moses*, and some other examples have been given in the preceding pages. Now, those works are commonly supposed by scholars to be Jewish and, if that is so, we are forced to say that the passage under discussion is a retouched form of an older Jewish formulation of these ideas. Alternatively, it may be the case that in light of passages like this one the presumed Jewish charater of the Adam books must be reconsidered and the possibility of a Christian sectarian origin entertained. Even then, the *Penitence of Adam* may be the repository of ancient Jewish traditions, a Jewish Adam book in Christian garb.

The Exculpation of Adam

Often, when the Latin text refers to Adam's sin, the Armenian text speaks of the loss of the paradisical food. This may be attempt to lighten the weight of Adam's sin, while highlighting Eve's role in it. This is clear in the example above drawn from chap. 3. At this point the Latin text is oddly repetitive and redundant, with Eve's saying the same thing twice, almost in the same words. The *Penitence of Adam*, however, is longer and much clearer. It expresses two ideas. The first is Eve's reaction of despair at their inability to find food. She states that she would prefer to die of hunger and anyway this might relieve Adam of his punishment, since she has been the cause of all the trouble. Adam denies, or at least raises a modicum of doubt about Eve's imputation of sin to herself. This does not daunt her and she then implores Adam to kill her, thus removing the source of the trouble. This time Adam does not challenge her imputation of sin to herself, but expresses his unwillingness to commit this great sin. Structurally the Armenian text appears to be much clearer than the Latin. Its climactic construction makes the point of Eve's sin inescapable and indeed the progression of her thought as outlined in this passage is itself obviously sinful and she has to be reproached by Adam.

In chap. 7 of the Latin *Vita Adae et Evae*, Adam stands up to his neck in water. This action, in fact, appertains to Eve and is part of Adam's instructions to her in chap. 6. In the Armenian *Penitence of Adam*, Adam goes to the river Jordan and the hair of his head was uncovered (see example from chap. 7, above). He then invokes the waters of the Jordan to gather all living things and let them stand around him (chap. 8). They gathered and were, according only to Armenian "like a wall". This obvious evocation of Exod. 14:22,29 (cf. Jos 3:13-17) implies that Adam in fact stood dry in the midst of the Jordan. This should be contrasted with what is said a little further on about Eve that her skin is wrinkled as a result of prolonged immersion in the water (thus the Armenian — Latin has: *de frigore aquae*) and she is so weakened by her acts of penitence that (again according only to the Armenian) she fell onto the ground in a faint for three days (chap. 10). Of Adam nothing similar is said. To the contrary the waters of the Jordan stand still, the living things form a wall around him and pray on his behalf. Again, the special status of Adam and the minimization of his culpability and therefore of his expiatory suffering are to be observed. It is intriguing to speculate about the relationship of these views to that of Adam's eschatological baptism in the Jordan.

These examples suffice to indicate the importance of the Armenian *Penitence of Adam* for the study of the versions of the Adam book. Indeed they indicate that the Armenian work may prove of crucial importance for recovery of certain structural, textual, literary and cultural aspects of that writing. The views highlighted here will prove of importance for the characterization of circles in which the Adam book was transmitted or composed.

The Translation

The translation is generally literal, subject always to the strictures of English style. The readings marked "lege" in the apparatus to the text are always included in the translation. Where, as often happens, the object which is a personal pronoun is not expressed by the Armenian text but is required in the translation by English usage, it is supplied with no further notation. All other supplements are marked by parentheses. The biblicizing (? Semiticizing) style of this writing leads it to start nearly every sentence with the word "and". This is mostly omitted in the translation. Otiose *kam* in double questions is also omitted with no notation. Participles of the Armenian are often rendered as finite verbs in English.

Pointed brackets enclose readings which have been accepted into the text from manuscripts other than MS A. Parentheses enclose words or phrases added by the editor for stylistic reasons and which do not reflect anything found in either the text or the apparatus.

Notes on the Translation

The notes cite parallels drawn from a broad range of biblical and extra-biblical writings. They make no claim to be exhaustive. In particular, much information may be found in L. Ginzberg, *Legends of the Jews*, 5.63-131. Only a selection from this rich treasure is cited.

ABBREVIATIONS USED IN THE NOTES
ON THE TRANSLATION

Abod Zar	Tractate Aboda Zara, Babylonian Talmud.
Adam Fg. I, II	Adam Fragments, see M.E. Stone, *Armenian Apocrypha relating to Patriarchs and Prophets*, Jerusalem: Israel Academy, 1981.
Apoc Paul	Apocalypse of Paul
Arm 4 Ezra	M.E. Stone, *Armenian Version of IV Ezra* (University of Pennsylvania Armenian Texts and Studies 1) Missoula: Scholars, 1979.
ARN	Abot de Rabbi Nathan, ed. S. Schechter, New York: Jewish Theological Seminary, 1967.
Aso Isa	Ascension of Isaiah.
Ber	Tractate Berakot, Babylonian Talmud.
Bib Ant	Pseudo-Philo, Liber Antiquitatum Biblicarum.
Book Adam	The Book of Adam, Issaverdens pp. 23-24.
Budge *Alexander*	E.A.W. Budge, *The Life and Exploits of Alexander the Great*, London: Clay, 1896.
Cain Abel	The History of Cain and Abel, Sons of Adam, Issaverdens pp. 53-58.
Conflict Christ Devil	See Vassiliev.
Creat Adam	History of the Creation and Transgression of Adam, Issaverdens pp. 43-48.
Death Adam	M.E. Stone, "The Death of Adam; An Armenian Adam Book", *HTR* 59 (1966), 283-291.
Deut R	Midrash Deuteronomy Rabba.
Expuls Adam	History of the Expulsion of Adam from the Garden, Issaverdens pp. 49-51.
Fuchs	C. Fuchs, "Das Leben Adam und Evas" *Die Apokryphen und Pseudepigraphen des Alten Testaments* ed. E. Kautzsch, repr; Darmstat: 1962, 2.506-528.
Gen R.	*Bereschit Rabba*, ed. J. Theodor, Jerusalem: Wahrmann, 1965.
Georg	W. Lüdtke, "Georgische Adam-Bücher", *ZAW* 38 (1919-20), 155-168.
Ginzberg *Legends*	L. Ginzberg, *Legends of the Jews*, Philadelphia; JPS, 1909-38, Vols. 1-7.
Good Tidings Seth	Concerning the Good Tidings of Seth, Issaverdens pp. 59-64.
Gosp Bartholemew	The Gospel of Bartholemew.
Gr.	Greek; The Apocalypse of Moses.
Hag	Tractate Haggiga, Babylonian Talmud.
Jos Ant	Josephus, *Antiquities of the Jews*

Jub	The Book of Jubilees.
Lat	Latin; the *Vita Adae et Evae*.
Lat MS	Latin Manuscript.
Lat I, II, III	Recensions of the Latin version.
Levene	Al Levene, *The Early Syriac Fathers on Genesis*, London: Taylors, 1951.
Malan	S.C. Malan, *The Book of Adam and Eve*, London: Williams & Northgate, 1882.
Matenadaran	Erevan, Matenadaran, Institute of Ancient Manuscripts, MS no...
Palaea	see Vassiliev.
Paralip Jer	The Paralipomena of Jeremiah.
Pes R	Midrash Pesiqta Rabbati.
Pseudo-Epiphanius *Hexameron*	E. Trumpp, *Das Hexaëmeron des Pseudo-Epiphanius* (Abh. kön. bayer. Akad. Wiss. Philos.-Philol. Class, 16.2) Munich: 1882.
Repent Adam	History of the Repentance of Adam and Eve, Issaverdens pp. 65-71.
Sanh	Tractate Sanhedrin, Babylonian Talmud.
Schatzhöhle	C. Bezold, *Die Schatzhöhle, 1, Übersetzung*, Leipzig: Hinrich, 1883.
Shab	Tractate Shabbat, Babylonian Talmud.
Slav	Slavonic; The Slavonic Life of Adam and.Eve.
Tanh	Midrash Tanhuma.
Tanh Buber	*Midrash Tanhuma*, ed. S. Buber.
Te'ezaza Sanbat	W. Leslau, *A Falasha Anthology*, New York: Schocken, 1969, 1-39.
Test Abraham	Testament of Abraham.
Test Adam	Testament of Adam.
Vaillant	A. Vaillant, *Le Livre des Secrets d'Hénoch*, Paris: Institut des Études Slaves, 1952.
Vassiliev	A. Vassiliev, *Anecdota Graeco-Byzantina*, Moscow: Imperial University, 1893.
Words Adam	Adam's Words to Seth, Issaverdens pp. 73-74.

THE PENITENCE OF <OUR> FOREFATHER ADAM[1]

1. It came to pass, when Adam went forth from the Garden with his
wife, outside, to the east[1] of the Garden, they made themselves a hut to
live in and went inside. Their tears fell ceaselessly and they spent their
5 days in unison of mind, weeping and saddened, and they said to one
another, "We are far from life." Then, after seven days,[2] they grew
hungry and looked for food.

2. Eve said to Adam. "My lord, I am hungry. Arise, seek food so that
we may live and know[1] that God is going to come and bring us to the
10 Garden, to our place." They arose and went about upon the earth, and
they did not find food like the food by which they had been nourished
<in the Garden>.

3. Eve said to Adam, "I am dying of this hunger. It would be better if
I were dead, my lord; perhaps (then) they would bring you into the
15 Garden, for because of me God is angry."[1] Adam said, "Great wrath has
come upon us, I know not whether because of you or because of me."
Eve said to h<im>, "Kill me if you wish, so that the wrath and anger
may abate from before you — for this has come about because of me —
and they will bring you into the Garden." Adam said to her. "Eve, do not
20 (even) mention this matter;[2] lest God bring upon us even greater evils
and we become contemptible. How, indeed, can I do you any evil, for
you are my body?"[3]

4. Eve[1] said "Arise, so that we may seek vegetable food." They
<sought> and they did not find <vegetable sustenance like that which
25 was in the Garden>. [Eve said[2] "...] because God established this
vegetable food as food for the beasts that they might eat on the earth, but
our food is that which the angels eat.[3] Arise, let us repent for forty days;

Title [1] Introduction pp. VIII-X; Lat MS 18 paenitentia Ad. et Ev.
    1. [1] Gen 3:24, Gr 1; contrast Malan 1:1, Pseudo-Epiphanius *Hexameron* 254 "west";
cf. PRE 20; see chap. 18 below. — [2] Lat, Slav 28, Creat Adam 47, Expuls Adam 51, Cain
Abel 53, Vat. Gr. no. 1192 13v; for variant "5" of MS C cf. Cain Abel 53, Death Adam 1
(but see variant there).
    2. [1] cf. Lat variant readings.
    3. [1] Introduction pp. XVI-XVII — [2] Contrast Slav 29. — [3] Gen 2:24.
    4. [1] Thus MS C; lacuna in MSS A and C; "vegetable sustenance" cf. Gen 1:30, Slav 30,
Levene 77, Sanh 59b, Gen R 20.9 (193f.). — [2] In Lat Adam is speaker. — [3] Ps 78:25. —

perhaps God will pity us and give <us> food which is better than that
of the beasts so that we should not become like them."[4]

Adam said to Eve, "In what fashion will you repent? How many days
can you endure toils? Perhaps you will begin and be unable to repent,
and God will not hearken, so that we will not be able to keep that which   5
we originally received."[5]

5. Eve said, "Set me the number of days which I might think to
repent; perhaps the days will be too long — for I brought this penitence
upon you".

6. Adam said, "You cannot endure the same number of days as I, but   10
do what I tell you and abide by <this> instruction". — Adam said, "I
shall be (in penitence) for forty days,[1] six days more than you, because
you were created on the sixth day[2] (of those upon which) he accepted his
works. Now, therefore, arise, go to the Tigris river and take a stone and
place it under your feet and stand in the water up to your neck, in your   15
clothes. Let no word of supplication to God escape your mouth, for we
are unworthy of <soul> and our lips are impure and unclean, because
of the transgressions which we committed in the Garden when we ate of
the tree. Stand silent there in the middle of the water until you have done
penitence for thirty four days, and I will be in the Jordan river,[3] until we   20
learn that, behold, God has hearkened to us and will give us our food".[4]

7. Then Eve went to the Tigris and did as Adam had instructed her,
and Adam went to the Jordan. And the hair of his head was uncovered.[1]

8. He prayed and said, "I say to you,[1] waters of Jordan, be fellow-
sufferers for me and assemble all the moving thing<s> which are in   25
you, and let them surround me and bewail me, not for their own sakes,
but for mine. Because God did not withhold their food from them, which
God appointed from the beginning, but I have been withheld from my
food and from life".[2]

When Adam said that, all moving things which were in the Jordan   30

---

[4] Contrast Lat; Gen R 20:9 (194), Te'ezaza Sanbat 15; PRE 19; cf. chap. 18 note c below.
— [5] i.e. "upon ourselves" cf. Lat 5.

6. Lat variants 36 and 40 days; Vat. Gr. no. 1192 13v 40 and 44 days; 34 and 40 days
Georg 158, Malan 1:32, 34; 30 days' mourning Gr MS B, Palaea 191, Matenadaran 2245
179r. — [2] Jub 3:4-6, Life of Adam (Syncellus, ed. Dindorf 6); "5th day" Georg 158. —
[3] PRE 20 "upper Gihon", cf. Gen 2:13f.; Malan 1:9-10, 32. — [4] Contrast Lat; Vat. Gr.
no. 1182 13v καὶ δώσει ἡμῖν τροφήν.

7. [1] Lat om; Vat. Gr. no. 1182 13v καὶ ἡ θρὶξ τῆς κεφαλῆς αὐτοῦ ἡπλοῦτου τῷ
εὐχομένῳ ἐν τῷ ὕδατι; Slav 36.

8. [1] Singular; number varies throughout chap. 8. — [2] Contrast Lat; Vat. Gr. no. 1182
om. —

gathered to him and stood around him like a wall.[3] And the waters of the Jordan stopped at that time and became stationary from their flow. Adam cried to God and he set apart six thousand orders of them[4] to call to God in prayers all the days.

5   **9.** When[1] eighteen days of their weeping were completed, then Satan took on the form of a cherub with splendid attire,[2] and went to the Tigris river to deceive Eve. Her tears were falling on her attire, down to the ground.

Satan said to Eve, "Come forth from the water and rest,[3] for God has
10 hearkened to your penitence, to you and Adam your husband. Because we beseeched God, God sent me to lead you forth from there and to give you your food, on account of which you repented. Since just now I went to Adam and he sent me to you and said, 'Go, son, summon my wife',[4] now come, let us go to Adam and I will lead you to the place where your
15 food is".

10. When Eve came forth from the water, her flesh was like withered grass, for her flesh had been changed from the water, but the form of her glory remained brilliant.[1] When she came forth from the water she fell down and remained upon the ground in great distress for two days, for
20 she was quite unable to move from the spot. Then she arose and Satan also led her to where Adam was. When Adam saw Satan and Eve who was following him, he wept loudly and called out with a great voice and said to Eve,

'Where is my command of repentance, which I gave you? How did you
25 go astray, to follow him by whom we were alienated from our dwelling?"

11. When Eve heard this, she knew that he who deceived her was Satan; she fell down before Adam. From that time Adam's distress increased twofold when he saw the sufferings of his wife, for she was overcome and fell like one dead. He was sad and called out great
30 lamentation and said to Satan, "Why have you engaged in such a great conflict with us? What are our sins against you, that you have brought us out of our place? Did we take your glory from you? Did we reject you from being our possession,[1] that you fight against us unnecessarily?"

---

[3] Lat om; Vat. Gr. no. 1182 14r ἐκύκλωσαν τὸν Ἀδὰμ ὡς τεῖχος κύκλῳ αὐτοῦ, cf. Exod 14:22, 29, Slav 37. — [4] No parallels known.

9. [1] Lat; Slav 39 reverses story of chaps. 10-11. — [2] Cf. 2 Cor 11:14, Gr 17, Slav 38, Malan 1:27, 28, 33. — [3] Lat variant reading. — [4] Malan 1:33; Lat om.

10. [1] Tanh Buber 1.7r-v, Gen R 12:6 (102), Pes R 118r; see Ginzberg *Legends* 5.112f., Adam Fg. I.2, Words Adam 3, Creat Adam 46, Gosp. Bartholemew 4; cf. PRE 20 on Adam; Budge *Alexander* 269.

11. [1] Translation after N. Bogharian.

12. Satan also wept loudly and said to Adam, "All my arrogance and sorrow came to pass because of you; for, because of you I went forth from my dwelling; and because of you I was alienated from the throne of the cherubs who, having spread out a shelter, used to enclose me; because of you my feet have trodden the earth".[1] Adam replied and said 5 to him, "What are our sins[2] against you, that you did all this to us?

13. Satan replied and said, "You did nothing to me, but I came to this measure because of you, on the day on which you were created, for I went forth on that day. When God breathed his spirit into you, you received the likeness of his image.[1] Thereupon, Michael came and made 10 you bow down before God. God said to Michael, 'Behold I have made Adam in the likeness of my image'.

14. Then Michael summoned all the angels, and God said to them, 'Come, bow down to god[1] whom I made'.

Michael bowed first. He called me and said, 'You too, bow down to 15 Adam'.

I said, 'Go away, Michael! I shall not bow down to him who is posterior to me, for I am former. Why is it proper for me to bow down to him?'[2]

15. The other angels, too, who were with me, heard this, and my 20 words seemed pleasing to them and they did not prostrate themselves to you, Adam.[1]

16. Thereupon, God became angry with me and commanded to expel us from our dwelling and to cast me and my angels,[1] who were in agreement with me, to the earth; and you were at the same time in the 25 Garden. When I realized that because of you I had gone forth from the dwelling of light and was in sorrows and pains, then I prepared a trap for you, so that I might alienate you from your happiness just as I, too, had been alienated because of you".[2]

17. When Adam heard this, he said to the Lord, "Lord, my soul is in 30

---

12. [1] Fall of Satan, cf. Isa 14:12-15; citation and analysis of sources Ginzberg *Legends* 5.84-86; see also Creat Adam 43, Malan 1:6,13, Vat. Gr. no 1192 17v seqq., Vat. Gr. no. 1190 882v seqq., Cod. Nazareus 65 apud Meyer Lat; cf. Schatzhöhle 4. — [2] MSS A C corrupt, emend to *մեղանր* (cf. chap. 11, below) or *մեղր*.

13. [1] Gen 1:26f, 2:7.

14. [1] MS C "to Adam"; Lat adorate imaginem dei; perhaps "image" lost by MS A, and MS C is a correction; cf. chap. 13, below; conflict Sammael and Michael PRE 27. — [2] Conflict Christ Devil 6.

15. [1] Lat varies; Arm om reference to Isa 14:14.

16. [1] Lat II, III; contrast PRE 14, 27. — [2] Chap. 47(39), Death Adam 5.

your hand. Make this enemy of mine distant from me, who desires to lead me astray, I who am searching for the light that I have lost".[1]

At that time Satan passed away from him. Adam stood from then on in the waters of repentance,[2] and Eve remained fallen upon the ground for three days, like one dead. Then, after three days,[3] she arose from the earth, and she said to Adam,

18. "You are innocent of the first sin and of this second one. Only me alone did Satan overcome, as a result of God's word and yours".[1] Again Eve said to Adam, "Behold, I shall go to the west[2] and I shall be there and my food (will be) grass until I die; for henceforth I am unworthy of the foods of life".[3]

Eve went to the west and she mourned and was sad; and then she made a hut for herself in the west, and she was advanced in her pregnancy[4] and she had Cain, the lawless one, in her womb.

19. When the times of her parturition came, she began to cry out in a loud voice and said,

"Where is Adam, that he might see this pain of mine? Who, indeed will relate my afflictions to Adam? Is there a wind under the heavens that will go and tell Adam, 'Come and help Eve!'?" And she said, "I implore you, all luminaries, when you come to the east, tell my lord Adam about my pains".[1]

20. Then Adam, in the river Jordan,[1] heard Eve's cry and her weeping. When God hearkened to the sound of Adam's penitence, he taught him sowing and reaping and that which was to come upon him and his seed.[2] Then Adam heard the sound of Eve's entreaty in the west, and Adam said to himself,[3]

"That voice and weeping are of my flesh. Let me arise and go to her

---

17. [1] Malan 1:14, Adam Fg. 1.4, Expuls Adam 50; Lat has "glory" here and elsewhere, cf. Words Adam 3. — [2] Lat om to end of chap. — [3] Paralip Jer 9:7-26, Asc Isa Gr (von Gebhardt, *ZWT* 21 [1870] 330ff.); Test Abraham A 20; W. Bousset, *Die Himmelreise der Seele* (repr; Darmstatd: 1960) 24ff., 63.

18. [1] i.e. God's command about the tree; Adam's about repentance. — [2] See chap. 1 note 1, chap. 20; Greek 1; "east" Georg 158. — [3] See chap. 4 note d, Adam Fg. I.9, Words Adam 13. — [4] Literally "extended by months".

19. [1] Death Adam 5, Malan 1:74, Georg 158; cf. Gen 3:16.

20. [1] Cf. chap. 7 and Lat 17, 20; Lat is shorter. — [2] Resolution of the quest for food and penitence, cf. Lat 22, Gr 29 and chap. [44](29) note 3; similar Georg 158, Creat Adam 47; comparable "Prometheus" traditions about Adam, see Ginzberg *Legends* 5. 105f., Gen R 24:7 (236), Slav 32, Death Adam 3; contrast Jub 3:35; the future is revealed to Adam after repentance Test Adam (Renan, JA 17 [1853] 5), Schatzhöhle 7. — [3] Literally "in his heart".

24(5) Then, after that, he had sons and daughters, thirty of each kind,[1] and they grew up.[2]

30(5) Adam was upon the earth nine hundred and thirty years,[1] and then Adam fell sick with a mortal affliction,[2] and he cried out in a loud voice and said,   5

"Let all my sons come and gather by me, so that I may see them first, before I die".

All his sons who were in every part of the world gathered by him. They assembled by him inside the place which Eve[3] had entered, and he prayed to the Lord God.   10

31(6) His son Seth said to Adam, "My father, did you remember the fruit of the Garden, of which you used to eat,[1] and have you become sad from that longing? If indeed this is the case, tell me, so that I may go close to the Garden and cast dust[2] upon my head and weep. For, perhaps God will give me of the fruit, that I might bring (it) to you, and this pain   15 may be driven away from you".[3]

Adam said to him, "It is not so, my son, Seth; rather do I have mortal sickness and pain".

Seth said to him, "Through whom did this pain come to you?"

32(7) Adam said to him, "When God made us, me and your mother,[1]   20 he gave us a command not to eat of that tree.[2] Satan deceived us at the hour when the angels who were guardians of the tree ascended to worship God.[3] Then, Satan caused Eve to eat that fruit; Eve caused me, who did not know, to eat it.[4]

32. For, my son Seth, God divided the Garden between me and your   25 mother Eve, that we might watch it.[1] To me he gave the eastern portion and the northern,[2] and to your mother, the western and the southern.

33. We had twelve[1] angels who went around with each of us, because of the guarding of the Garden, until the time of the light.

24(5) [1] Gen 5:4, etc.; Book Adam 24 has "30 sons", cf. Repent Adam 69. — [2] Or "they increased" cf. Lat.

30(5) [1] Gen 5:5, Jub 4:29, Jos Ant 1.67, etc.; cf. 900 in Death Adam Superscription, 10. — [2] Some Gr MSS om this phrase; in general cf. Schatzhöhle 9, Malan 2:8. — [3] "Eve" may result from dittography here.

31(6) [1] Gen 2:16, 3:2. — [2] So Lat, Book Adam 26, Gr 7, Lat 36, etc.; "dung" Gr. — [3] Lat om this phrase.

32(7) [1] + "through whom I am dying" Gr; Arm differs variously in this chap. — [2] Gen 2:17, 3:3, 11. — [3] Test Adam (*Patrol. Syr.* 2) 1321-8 and parallels; Apotelesmata Apollonii Tyanensis (ibid) 1376; Test Abraham B 4; Apoc Paul 8. — [4] Gen 3:1-6.

32. [1] Gen 2:15, PRE 12. — [2] In MS A "northern" and "southern" are transposed; see Lat, Gosp Bartholemew 4:5.

33. [1] "2" Lat, cf. Hag 16r *et al.*

33(7) Since, every day they would go forth to worship the Lord, at the time when they went to the heavens, at that time Satan deceived your mother and caused her to eat of the fruit. Satan knew that I was not with her,[1] nor the angels,[2] at that time he caused her to eat. Afterwards, also,
5 she gave it to me.

34(8) I knew then, when I ate the fruit, that God was angry with us.[1]

God said, 'Because you transgressed my commandment,[2] I shall bring seventy afflictions upon your body, pain of the eyes and ringing of the ears[3] and all the joints'.

10 It will be reckoned for me (?) among the afflictions of sickness which are preserved in the treasuries, so that God might send them in the last times".[4]

35(9) When Adam said this to his son Seth, he cried out and said, "What shall I do, for I am in great pains and toils". Eve wept and said,
15 "My lord Adam. Arise, give me some of your pain, so that I might receive and bear it, for these pains which have come upon you, came about because of me".[1]

36(9) Adam said to her, "Arise, go with your[1] son Seth, close to the Garden and there cast dust on your heads and weep before God. Perhaps
20 God will pity me and send his angel to the Garden,[2] and he will go to the place where the olive-tree stands,[3] from which oil[4] comes forth, and give you a little of it, so that you might bring it to me and I might anoint my bones and be separated from pain, and I might teach you this way ... which we were tried formerly".[5]

25 **37**(10) Thereafter, Seth and Eve went in the direction of the Garden.

33(7) [1] Gen R 19:2 (171f.), ARN A1 (4). — [2] Creat Adam 44.

34(8) [1] Gen 3:7, 10. — [2] Gen 3:17. — [3] *ηῦ ȷgnρῦȷqnιῦu* doubtful; read as if from *ηῦηȷ* — "noise" and *nιῦιῆ* "ear"; ·*ȷn*· remain problematic. — [4] This sentence is not paralleled in Gr and Lat.

35(9) [1] Gen 3:17-19.

36(9) [1] meo Lat, ἡμῶν Gr, your Book Adam; derivative parallel story Acts Pilate Gr 3 and Lat B 4:3; parallel story Words Adam, Adam Fg. I, Adam Fg. II. — [2] ab arborem misericordiae Lat; Slav om "angel" here, but not in next chap. — [3] Not specifically an olive Lat, Gr; but cf. 2 Enoch 8:3 (Vaillant 9). — [4] See chap. 41(13), oleum vitae Lat; see also Ps.-Clem. *Recog.* 1.45.5, 2 Enoch 8:5 (Vaillant 9), 22:8-10 (Vaillant 26), 4 Ezra 2:12. — [5] "and I might teach you ... formerly" om Lat; it is slightly corrupt; ante-mortem revelation to Seth Test Adam (*Patrolog. Syr.* 2) 1329f., 1343-6, etc.; see further Stone *Patriarchs and Prophets* 46-48 (forthcoming); CG V. 5 is also a testamentary revelation by Adam to Seth, see LXX Gen 5:3-4, see chap. [44](30) and [23](3) note 4:*ȷnȷȷ*"way" here corresponds to Gr τρόπον, although it usually means "proverb"; like here Arm 4 Ezra 4:3 = Lat via; with slight emendation the last verb might be "tempted".

was guarding the lot of his portion which had been given to him by God[3] and I was guarding in my lot, at the southern and western side, Satan[4] went to your father's lot, where the wild beasts[5] were. He summond the serpent and said to him, 'Arise, come to me!' For God had divided the wild beasts and given them to us — the male ones he gave to your father 5 and the female ones he gave to me. We used to nourish them according to whichever of us it had been allotted.[6]

[**44**](16) Satan said to the serpent, 'Arise, come to me and I will tell you something which is of profit to you'.

Then the serpent came to him and Satan said to it, "I hear that you are 10 wiser than all the wild animals[1] and I have come to see you. I found that there is none like you in your cunning among all the animals. Even[2] as Adam gave nourishment to all the wild beasts, so also you did."[3]

And then, when the wild beasts went to worship Adam, Satan went with them and said to the serpent,   15

'Why do you worship Adam every morning? You came into being before him: why is it that you, who are the former one, worship the later? Rather should the younger worship the older.[4] Why do you worship (Adam) or (why) are you fed by Adam and are not fed by the fruit of the Garden? Come on, rise up, come to me and hear what I say to 20 you. Let us expel Adam from the Garden like us[5] so that we may re-enter the Garden'.[6]

The serpent said, 'In what way or how can we expel him from the Garden?'[7]

Satan said to the serpent, 'Be you, in your form, a lyre for me and I 25 will pronounce speech through your mouth, so that we may be able to help.'[8]

[**44**](17) Then the two of them came to me and hung their feet around the wall of the Garden. When the angels ascended to the worship of the Lord,[1] at that time Satan took on the form of an angel and began to 30

---

[3] διάβολος Gr here and following; cf. Jos Ant 1.4. — [4] Gen 2:15; chap. 32 above, Lat 32; cf. Gosp Bartholemew 4:5. — [5] τὰ ἀρσενικὰ θηρία Gr; Schatzhöhle 6. — [6] Arm rough here; καὶ ἕκαστος ἡμῶν τὰ ἑαυτοῦ ἐτήρει Gr.

44(16) [1] Gen 3:1, Creat Adam 44, Schatzhöhle 6, Malan 1:17, Gen R 19:1 (171), PRE 13. — [2] Gr is much shorter, perhaps abbreviated. — [3] Idea not in Gr, cf. Malan 1:17. — [4] Cf. chap. 14; not in Gr, but by Gr phrase ὅμως προσκυνεῖς τὸν ἐλαχιστότερον which is not glossed from Lat, *pace* Wells. — [5] Cf. chaps 12-16. — [6] Gr om last phrase. — [7] φοβοῦμαι μήποτε ὀργισθῇ μοι κύριος Gr. — [8] ἐξαπατῆσαι αὐτόν Gk; cf. in general PRE 13, Palaea 190 and chap. [44](17).

[**44**](17) [1] "sixth hour" Slav 7, cf. Test Adam (*Patrolog. Syr.* 2) 1325 etc., Apotelesmata Apollonii Tyanensis (ibid) 1378; "ninth" Gr MS C perhaps corrupt; Test Abraham B 4; Apoc Paul 7; Protoevang James 13. —

praise God with angelic praises. I knelt down by the wall and attended to his praises. I looked and saw him in the likeness of an angel;[2] when I looked again, I did not see him. Then he went and summoned the serpent and said to him,

5   'Arise, come to me so that I may enter into you and speak through your mouth as much as I will need say'.

At that time the serpent became a lyre for him,[3] and he came again to the wall of the Garden. He cried out and said,

'Oh, woman, you who are blind in this Garden of delight, arise come
10 to me and I will say some words to you'.

When I went to him, he said to me, 'Are you Eve?'

I said, 'Yes, I am'.

He replied and said, 'What do you do in < the Garden > ?'

I said to him, 'God set us to guard[4] the Garden',
15   Satan replied and said to me through the mouth of the serpent, 'This work is good, but come, do you eat of < all > the trees which are in the Garden?'

I said to him, 'Yes, we eat of all of them except only of that one tree which is in the very middle of the Garden, concerning which God
20 commanded us, "Do not eat of it, for if you eat you will surely die".'[5]

[**44.**](18) Then the serpent said, 'As the Lord lives, I am greatly concerned about you for you are like beasts,[1] since God has withheld (it) from you,[2] but I do not wish you to be ignorant. Come on, come and eat of the tree, and you see what honour will be yours'.
25   I said to him, 'I fear lest I die as God said to us'.

The serpent, together with Satan, replied and said to me, 'As the Lord lives, you (will) not die,[3] but when you eat, your eyes (will be) opened and you will become like God,[4] knowing good and evil. But God < knew > that you (will) become like him; he deceived you, that he said,
30 "Do not eat of it"'.[5] And he said, "Look at the tree and see what glory is around the tree"'.

When I looked at the tree, I saw (that) great glory was around it. I said to him,

'The tree is good and it looks pleasing to me,[6] but I cannot go and take

---

[2] Greek lacks up to 5. — [3] Cf. chap. 44(16). — [4] + "and to eat" Gr. — [5] Gen 2:17, 3:1-3, Jub 3:18.

[**44**](18) [1] cf. Ps 49:20, 4 Ezra 7:65-66, PRE 19. — [2] Gr om. — [3] Gr omits the element of dying. — [4] Plur Gr. — [5] Gen 2:17, 3:4-5, Jub 3:19, Jos Ant 1.42, Creat Adam, 44f., Palaea 190f. — [6] Gen 2:9, 3:6, Jub 3:20. —

of the fruit: I am afraid. Come here! If you are not afraid, bring me of the fruit and I will eat, so that I may know whether your words are true or not'.[7]

Then the serpent called to me and said, 'Come, open the gate for me and I will enter and I will give you of the fruit'. 5

[**44**](19) When he entered,[1] he proceeded a little way into the Garden and stopped,

I said, 'Why did you stop?'

He said to me, 'Perhaps, when I shall give you to eat and your eyes are opened and you become like God, you will deceive Adam and will not 10 give him to eat of the fruit and he will become like a beast before you.[2] But you, if you wish, swear to me truly that you will give him to eat, and will not deceive your husband Adam'.

I said to him, 'I do not know any oath by which I can swear to you, but I will say to you that which I do know: By the plants of the Garden and 15 by the Cherubs and the Seraphs and (by) the Father who sits in the heavens to descend to the Garden, if I eat and learn everything,[3] I shall not withhold, but I will give to my husband Adam to eat'.

When he had caught me through an oath, he then led me and brought me to the tree and he went forth to the tree. He set the deception in its 20 fruit,[4] that is desire of sins, harlotries, adulteries, greeds. He lowered[5] the branches of the tree to the earth. Then I took some of the fruit and I ate.[6]

[**44**](20) At that hour I learned with my eyes that I was naked of the glory[1] with which I had been clothed. Thenceforth, I began to weep and said, 25

'What did you do to me?'

<But I was no longer mortified about the war which (the) enemy had made against me;> then I learned, thenceforth, that he will lead me to the depths of hell.[2]

When Satan did this, he descended from the tree and hid in the 30 Garden.[3] In my parts of the Garden I sought leaves of a tree to cover my

---

[7] Gr shorter from "come here..." — end; ARN A1 (4); PRE 13, Palaea 190.

[**44**](19) [1] Literally "he came he entered" common hendyadis; Satan (Sammael) cannot enter the Garden Creat Adam 44, ARN A Appendix B (154). — [2] Sentence om Gr; cf. chap. [**44**](18). — [3] Phrase om Gr. — [4] Similar phrasing not idea Abod Zar 22b. — [5] "I lowered" Gr, but see Book Adam 30; cf. Gen R 19:3 (172), ARN A1 (4) — [6] Gen 3:6, Jub 3:20.

[**44**](20) [1] τῆς δικαιοσύνης Gk; Adam and Eve clothed with glory Yalqut Shim'oni Deut 951, Gen R 11:2 (88), PRE 14, Tanh on Gen 2:4, Creat Adam 45f. — [2] Gr varies. — [3] ἄφαντος ἐγένετο Gr. —

nakedness, and I could not find any on all the trees. For, at that hour all the trees of the Garden became leafless, except for the fig-tree alone. I took (its leaves) and covered my nakedness,[4] and I stood[5] by the tree of which I had eaten. I was afraid, my son Seth, because of the oath I swore that I would give my husband Adam to eat.

5   [44](21) I cried out to Adam in a loud voice, 'Arise, come to me and I will show you this way'.[1]

Then Adam came to me with his great glory, and I gave him to eat of the fruit, and I made him like me.[2] Subsequently, he, too, came (and) took a fig leaf and covered his nakedness.[3]

10   [44](22) After that, we heard the angel Gabriel[1] blowing a trumpet and summoning all the angels and saying to them,

'Thus[2] says the Lord, "Come to me so that I may descend to the Garden with you, and listen to my judgement with which I will judge Adam'".

15   When we heard the sound of the angel's trumpet, we knew that God was about to come to the Garden to judge us.[3] He set forth upon upon the Cherub chariot and the angels were praising him; consequently, we were afraid and hid.[4] God reached the Garden and all of the plants of the garden flowered. He set up his throne < close > to the tree of life.

20   [44](23) God summoned Adam and said, 'Adam, where are you?[1] Do you think that you have hidden and do you say, "He does not know me"? Can the building hide from the Builder, that you hide near that olive-tree?"[2]

Adam replied and said, 'No, Lord, it is not that having hidden, I think 25 that you will not find me, but I was afraid, for I am naked and I am ashamed.'[3]

God said to him, 'Who showed you to be naked, if you have not abandoned my commandment which I gave you to observe?"[4]

Then Adam remembered the injunction[5] which He had spoken to him, 30 to do and observe.[6] Adam said,

---

[4] Cf. Gen 3:7, Jub 3:21, Jos Ant 1.44, Creat Adam 46. — [5] ἐστίν Gk; Arm from ἔστην; the tree was a fig Gen R 15:7 (140), cf. Creat Adam 46, Schatzhöhle 6.

[44](21) [1] Or "parable", see chap. 36(9) note 5; μέγα μυστήριον Gr. — [2] Gr longer here. — [3] Gen 3:7, Jub 3:22, Jos Ant 1.44, PRE 13; Gr varies.

[44](22) [1] μιχαήλ Gr. — [2] Arm punctuation has been changed in accordance with Gr. — [3] 1 Thess 4:16, 'Otot Mašiaḥ (Jellinek, Bet Ha-Midrasch 2.6); PRE 14. — [4] Gen 3:8, Jos Ant 1.45.

[44](23) [1] Gen 3:9, Creat Adam 46; to this and chap. [44](24) cf. Jos Ant 1.44-49. — [2] Gr om this phrase. — [3] Gen 3:10, Creat Adam 46. — [4] Gen 3:11. — [5] Or "word". — [6] Gen 2:16; Gr and Book Adam differ, referring to Eve's deceit. —

'This woman, whom you gave, deceived me and I ate'.[7]

He <turned> to me and said, 'Why did you do that?'

I recalled the serpent's speech and said, 'The serpent deceived me'.[8]

[44](24) Subsequently God said to Adam, 'Because you obeyed your wife's voice and transgressed my commandment, you will be condemned   5 upon the earth. You will toil upon it, <and it will not give you its strength> ;[1] thorns and <thistles> will sprout forth[2] for you. By the sweat of your brow you shall eat your bread[3] and you shall have no rest; you <shall hunger> and you shall be sated[4] and you shall be afflicted by bitterness then you shall eat of[5] sweetness; you shall be tormented by   10 heat and afflicted by cold; you shall be pauperized and become great;[4] <you shall grow fat and you will be weakened and> the beasts <which> you ruled will rise up against you malignantly, because you transgressed my commandment and did not observe (it)'.

[44](25) God turned and said to me, 'Because you obeyed the serpent   15 <and transgressed my commandment> you shall suffer torments and pains.[1] You shall bear many children and at the time of birth <you shall bring> your life <to an end> and, from your great agonies and pains you shall promise with your mouth and say, "If I survive these agonies, I shall never go back to my husband".[2] And when you emerge from the   20 agonies, you shall return immediately to the earth. For you shall be condemned by your own mouth,[3] since you promised when the pain was acute, "I will never go back to this earth" and then you returned to the same. In pain you shall bear children and in pity you shall return to your husband and he will rule over you'.[4]   25

[44](26) After he had said all this to me, the Lord became very angry at the serpent and said,

'Because you did this and became a lyre <to lead astray those who were weak[1] of heart>, be cursed more than all the animals.[2] Be withheld from your foods which you used to eat. Dust will be your food and you   30 shall go upon your breast and your stomach;[3] your feet and hands will be withheld and your <ears> will not hear, <and none of your limbs.[4]

---

[7] Gen 3:12, Creat Adam 46. — [8] Gen 3:13, Creat Adam 47.

[44](24) [1] Gen 3:17. — [2] Gen 3:18, Creat Adam 47. — [3] Gen 3:19, Jub 3:25, Creat Adam 47. — [4] Negative in Greek. — [5] Gr is shorter.

[44](25) [1] Creat Adam 47. — [2] This corresponds to Gr "sin of the flesh" cf Gen 3:16c. — [3] From here to "in pity", Gr has διὰ τὴν ἔχθραν ὃν ἔθετο ὁ ἐχθρὸς ἐν σοί. — [4] Gen 3:16.

[44](26) [1] Participle. — [2] Gen 3:14a-b. — [3] Gen 3:14b. — [4] Gr om from here to "your heart"; Jos Ant 1.50f., Apoc. Abraham 23, Targum J. to Gen 3:14, Gen R 19:1, 20:5 (171, 186), Yalqut Shim'oni 3:31, ARN B 42 (59), et al., Schatzhöhle 7, PRE 13, 14. —

A likeness of the cross will bring my son to the earth, because of him whom you deceived. Be disabled and broken because of the evil of your heart. I have set enmity between you and Adam's seed. You will lie in wait for his heel and he for your head,[5] until the day upon which you will
5 be punished'.

[**44**](27) When God had said this, he commanded our expulsion from the Garden, and the angels set about expelling us.[1] Adam beseeched the angels and said,

'Let me be for a little, so that I may beseech God about my sins.
10 Perhaps he will grant me penitence and not expel (me) from the Garden'.

The angels let him be from expelling (him) from the Garden, and Adam said,

'Be gracious to me, Lord God, for I have sinned against you'.[2]

Then the Lord said [to the angels], 'Do not let him stand still, but expel
15 (him) from the Garden. Were the sins mine? Do I pronounce judgement in vain?'

Then the angels worshipped God and said, 'You are just, O Lord, and your judgements are upright'.

[**44**](28) Adam said again[1] to God, 'My Lord, I beseech you, give me
20 of the tree of life, so that I may eat before I shall have gone forth from the Garden'.

God said to Adam, 'You cannot take of it in your lifetime, because I have given an order to the Seraphs to guard it round about with weapons because of you,[2] lest you should eat more of it and become immortal and
25 say, "Behold, I shall not die"; and you will be boastful of it[3] and be victorious in the war which the enemy has made with you. Rather, when you go out of the Garden, guard yourself from slander, from harlotry, from adultery, from sorcery, from the love of money, from avarice and from all sins.[4] Then, you shall arise from death, (in the) resurrection
30 which is going to take place.[5] At that time, I will give you of the tree of life and you will be eternally undying'.[6]

[**44**](29) When God had said this, he commanded to expel us from the Garden. Adam began to cry before the angels, and the angels said to him,

'What do you want us to do for you?'

---

[5] Gen 3:17, Creat Adam 47; Gr om last phrase.
   [**44**](27) [1] Creat Adam 47. — [2] See chaps. 4, 18, 21 above.
   [**44**](28) [1] Or "Adam turned and said". — [2] Gen 3:24, Gr χερουβίυ and closer to Gen; Creat Adam 47. — [3] Gr om this phrase. — [4] Gr just ἀπὸ παντὸς κακοῦ. — [5] Gen 42:13, Gen R 20:10 (194), Ber 5a. — [6] Gen 3:22.

Adam replied and said to the angels,[1] 'I beseech you, let(me) be a little, so that I may take sweet incenses with me from the Garden, so that when I go out of here, I may offer sweet incenses to God, and offerings, so that, perhaps, God will hearken to us'.[2]

The angels let him be, and he took sweet incenses with him, iris and   5 balsam.[3] We took them and went forth from the Garden to this land.

[44](30) Now, my son, Seth,[1] I have shown you the way, how we sinned. But you, take care to do the good things. Do not abandon[2] God's command and do not depart from his mercy. Behold, I will show you every sort of recompense, both of good and of evil. > "   10

45(31) At the time when Adam was ill and they were standing around him, because one more day remained of his life and Adam's soul was going forth from his body, Eve related all this. And again Eve said to Adam,

"Why do you die and I live? Tell me, what shall I do for you? How 15 long shall I be on the earth after your death?

Adam said to her, "Do not concern yourself with earthly things, but consider that we will both die as a couple, and they will place you where I will be. But when I die, do not come near me to move me from the place, until God[1] speaks with you about me. For God will not forget me, but he 20 seeks the vessel which he made.[2] Now, arise, pray to God until I give up my soul, which he gave me, into his hands. For I do not know how we shall preserve[3] for the Father of all, whether he will be angry or will be merciful to us".

46(32) Then Eve arose, beseeched God and said, "I have sinned, 25 God; I have sinned against you, my beloved Lord; I have sinned against your elect angels; I have sinned against the Cherubs;[1] I have sinned against the Seraphs; I have sinned before you, Lord.[2] I beseech all (you) whom God created in the heavens and on the earth, that you intercede with the Father in heaven".[3]   30

---

[44](29) [1] See chap. [44](27), Slav 25-27, Gr 21. — [2] Gr has additional sentence here. — [3] Arm forms are unusual and were identified by N. Bogharian; Gr has more spices, cf. Song 4:13-14; Gr adds καὶ λοιπὰ σπέρματα εἰς διατθοφὴν αὐτοῦ, cf. chap. 20, above, Lat 43, Jub 3:27; see Ginzberg Legends 5.105; contrast Gen R 20:10 (193f.), Schatzhöhle 8, Malan 1:30f., Test Adam, (Patrolog. Syr. 2) 1345, 1352.

[44](30) [1] Gr τεκνία μου; see chaps [23](3) note 4, 36(9) note 5. — [2] Gr om from here to end.

45(31) [1] ἄγγελος κυρίου Gr. — [2] Gen R 20:8 (194). — [3] Unclear; ἀπαντήσωμεν Gr.

46(32) [1] Gr longer. — [2] + καὶ πᾶσα ἁμαρτία δι' ἐμοῦ γέγονεν ἐν τῇ κτίσει Gr, cf. Slav. — [3] Gr om this sentence. —

While Eve was praying on bended knee, behold, the archangel Michael[3] came to her, stood her up and said,

"Arise, Eve, from your penitence. Behold, the soul of your husband Adam has gone forth from the body".[4]

47(38) Eve[1] arose, and all the angels assembled before her, each according to his rank.[2] Some of them bore censers in their hands, others bore trumpets and others bore blessings.[3] Behold, the Lord of hosts upon a Cherub chariot[4] and four <winds> were drawing him, and Cherubs were serving those winds and the angels were proceeding before him: God came to the earth, to the place where Adam's body lay, and all of the angels (were) before him with praises. God came to the Garden and all the plants <moved>, and all the people who were with Adam fell asleep. Only Seth alone, the virtuous one,[5] was awake, according to God's direction.

[**47**](39) God came to Adam's body, where he was lying dead. God[1] mourned greatly and said in a sweet voice,

"Oh, Adam. Why did you do that? If you had observed my commandment, those who brought you down to this place would not have rejoiced over you. But I will turn their rejoicing into sorrow, and I will turn your sorrow into rejoicing. I shall make you the beginning of rejoicing and I shall set you on the throne of him who deceived you,[2] and I shall cast them into a place of darkness and death".[3]

48(40) After this, God spoke to Michael and said, "Go to the Garden of the third heaven and bring me three linen cloths".

When he had brought them, God said to Michael and to Ozēl[1] and to Gabriel,[2]

"Bring these linen cloths and cover Adam's body, and bring sweet oil".

They brought them and set them around him and wound him in that garment. When they had finished everything, God ordered them to bring Abel's body. They brought still <other> linen cloths and dressed him. For he had remained from <that> day upon which Cain the lawless one[3] had killed him and had wished to hide him, and had been unable. For, as soon as his body was in the dust, a heavenly voice came[4] and said,

---

[4] Gr om name; "the Lord" Slav.

47(38) [1] Scope and order, cf. Lat; Gr longer. — [2] Angels before God Gr; om Lat. — [3] Gr om this sentence. — [4] Cf. Gr; Ps 18:10, PRE 4. — [5] Unusual form.

47(39) [1] ὁ Σήθ Gr. — [2] Isa 14:13, Jer 31:13b etc. — [3] Gr longer; Georg varies 160.

48(40) [1] Οὐριήλ + Ῥαφαήλ Gr. — [2] Yalqut Teh 889, Deut R 11 (end). — [3] ὁ ἀδελφὸς αὐτοῦ Gr. — [4] Literally "came about". —

"It is not permitted to hide him <in> the earth <before> the first creature has returned to the earth from which he came".

Thenceforth, they took him into that same cave⁵ where he was until Adam died. Then, after this, they brought him and treated him just as they had treated his father Adam. After the dressing, God commanded 5 that both of them be taken to the region of the Garden and be brought to the place from which the dust had been taken and Adam created.⁶ God caused them to dig in that place and sent them to bring sweet incenses and iris⁷ incense and he caused them to put oils upon the dust and to cover the spices.⁸ Then after this, they took the bodies of both of them 10 and put them in the place in which he had fashioned them.⁹ They exchanged¹⁰ and made a sepulchre over them.

[**48**](41) God called to Adam's body through the dust and said, "Adam, Adam".

Adam's body said to the dust, "Answer and say, 'Here (I am), Lord' ". 15

The Lord said to him, "Behold, just as I said to you, 'Adam, you are dust and you return to dust';¹ but I will raise you² in the resurrection which I promised you".

48(42) After God had said this, he took a three-fold seal¹ and sealed Adam's tomb and said,   20

"Let none approach in these days, until their bodies² return to it".

Then, at that time, the Lord ascended to the heavens with his angels, Seraphs and chariot of light, each to his station. The times of Eve were filled and completed and she was dying. She began to weep and sought to know the place where Adam was buried, because she was ignorant (of 25 it).³ For, at the time when God came for the death of Adam, all the plants of the Garden were moved and, through the holy spirit, sleep overcame all those who were upon the earth, until they had dressed Adam, and none upon the earth knew, except Seth alone.

Again Eve began to cry out, to beseech God that they should bring her 30

---

⁵ "Rock" Gr, Georg 160; Georg shorter; place of burial Aptowitzer, *Kain u. Abel* (Wien & Leipzig: 1922) 52-56; Cain Abel 58 cf. Repent Adam 67, Malan 1:79. — ⁶ Gr differs in this section. — ⁷ Reading Չորեկ (N. Bogharian). — ⁸ Schatzhöhle 9, Malan 2:9. — ⁹ Adam's burial Ginzberg *Legends* 5. 125f., cf. Jub 4:29, 2 Enoch Appendix 36 (Vaillant 117), Conflict Christ Devil 5, Gen R 14:8 (132), Malan 3:17, Repent Adam 71, Schatzhöhle 4, Death Adam 39. — ¹⁰ Probably corrupt for փորեցին "they dug".

48(41)   Gen 3:19, Words Adam 74. —   + μετὰ παντὸς ἀνθρώπου τοῦ ἐκ σπέρματός σου Gr, cf. Slav 47, Gen R 20:8 (194).

48(42) ¹ Shab 55a, cf. Kahana *ad loc.* — ² ἡ πλευρα αὐτοῦ Gr, cf. Slav 45. — ³ Gr variant and longer to end, Lat shorter. —

to the place where Adam was buried. When she had completed that prayer, she said,

"My God, God of miracles, do not alienate me from Adam's place, but command to place me in his tomb. Just as we were together in the
5 Garden, and were not separate from one another, just as in life, so in <our> death. In the place in which Adam was buried let me, too, be buried with him".[4]

50(42) When, beseeching, she had said this, her soul left her. Michael, the archangel, came and spoke to Seth and taught him how to dress her.[1]
10 Three angels came and took Eve's body and brought it and placed it where Adam's and Abel's bodies were.

48(43) After this, Michael spoke to Seth and said, "Thus shall you dress every human being who dies, until the day of the end, through the resurrection".
15   When the angel had said this to Seth,[1] he ascended to heaven, praising the Father and the Son and the Holy Spirit, now and for ever.

---

[4] Repent Adam 71, Death Adam 78.
  48(43) [1] Death Adam 78.
  50(42) [1] Slav 49-50.

I. INDEX OF PROPER NAMES

II. INDEX OF MODERN AUTHORS

CONTENTS